Every Child Is A Greening Valley

Meditations Of Encouragement
For Christian Teachers

By Dr. Richard Andersen

C.S.S. Publishing Company, Inc.
Lima, Ohio

EVERY CHILD IS A GREENING VALLEY

Library of Congress Cataloging-in-Publication Data
Andersen, Richard, 1931-
   Every child is a greening valley : stories for encouragement for
Christian teachers / by Richard Andersen
      p.   cm.
  ISBN 1-55673-298-8
   1. Teachers—Prayer-books and devotions—English. 1. Title.
BV4596.T43A53   1991
242'.69—dc20
                                                 90-21721
                                                   CIP

9129 / ISBN 1-55673-298-8

With appreciation to Jaroslav Vajda,
Al Senske,
and the staff of St. Timothy's School.

Preface

In recent years, three different devotional books for teachers were written and published. Jaroslav Vajda and Al Senske worked together in developing the idea I proposed, and the wonderful result was a series of bestsellers for Concordia Publishing House. I am hopeful that this book will prove as useful as the others and find its way into the hands of staff members in our Christian schools. While it is focused more on day school staffs, it is useful for Christian teachers involved in public schools and Sunday schools.

I am grateful to many people for their words of encouragement, as well as ideas they've offered. May God bless you in your ministry of educating others in the joy of Jesus Christ.

Joyously in Jesus,
The Author

Table of Contents

Samuel

A Rare Call

Now the boy Samuel was ministering to the Lord under Eli. And the word of the Lord was rare in those days; there was no frequent vision. — 1 Samuel 3:1-2

And Samuel grew, and the Lord was with him and let none of his words fall to the ground.
— 1 Samuel 3:19

Ryan was but three, a small boy with a determined spirit. One lustrous spring day, when his grandmother was looking out the front door window at the lad playing in the yard, she was shocked to see that he had grabbed all her bright blossoming daffodils, yanking them from their stems.

"Ryan," she called in her frustration, "What are you doing?"

"I told you," he asserted with impish savior-faire, "I don't like yellow."

Samuel, called by God, answered differently. "Speak, Lord, for thy servant hears," he said as the Eternal Father beckoned him. He had no color preference, no rebel yell to sound, no sense of his own importance. But he also had determination. It was to hear and heed that spine-tingling voice.

Hannah, his mother, in begging God for a son, promised to "give him to the Lord all the days of his life," a promise which she carried out faithfully. Samuel, too, was responsive to that promise. Instead of pulling up daffodils, he sought to plant ideas that, like seeds, would not only flower but bear a harvest. No wonder "none of his words [fell] to the ground." They were plucked like ripe olives from the trees of truth he cultivated. His was a career of harvesting the richness of God's message.

The classroom may seem like a farm that's always being planted, but seldom harvested. Like Ryan, we may decide

9

against the blossom because it's not our shade. Yet, if, like Samuel, we respond to the voice that emanates from dreams as well as daffodils, from visions of hope as well as the words of Scripture, will we not only see the bloom but also the bounty?

Samuel had the advantage of a believing mother, Hannah, and a faithful tutor, Eli. They prepared him for more than spring's buds, for the fruit which blossoms promise. He became the stalwart reformer, always faithful to the truth God voiced, and ever mindful of the harvest. Israel, weak in faith, and floundering against the might of her enemies, had been ripping out the daffodils without seeing them as harbingers of a greater future. They gave in to discontent too readily, only to have their dislike for the yellow they ripped out set before them for what it was: cowardice bereft of faith.

No wonder Samuel's words never fell to the ground. He held them up for people to see and savor, and in the process they both heard and saw God granting them the victory. Moses delivered God's people, but Samuel restored them from the weaklings they had become to a fruitful nation of believers.

While there may be some temporary satisfaction in uprooting sights that don't please us, Samuel demonstrates that we may be able to transform the present weaknesses into the power of God if we remain faithful, letting none of God's Words fail to produce the intended harvest. Samuel shows the reason for letting flowers evolve into fruit.

Mountains Of Work

Mountain, *n. Any part of a land mass which projects conspicuously above its surroundings; pl. a row or group of such elevations.*

And if I have prophetic powers, and understand all mysteries and all knowledge, and if I have all faith, so as to remove mountains, but have not love, I am nothing. — *1 Corinthians 13:2*

My desk is like the Dolomites. Jagged and ragged towering clumps of papers and books, piercing Matterhorn-like pencils in a holder, and stacked audio and video tapes that resemble Ship Rock and Half Dome (depending on the perspective), and a marble desk stand looking like a slice of the Grand Canyon with its golden calendar a sunrise ever dawning, occupy my working space.

A child once commented that she had seen something like it. It was a picture of the Grand Tetons. She asked what I did with the lake. A bowl of blue water I had used for an object lesson, and discarded, once set before this monstrous mountain range. She knew the Grand Tetons couldn't exist without Jackson Lake. My desk represents mountains of work, the Rockies unscaled, Kilamanjaro ignored.

The problem is that I have a mountain range on top of my desk, as well as one beneath that dwarfs Everest in its scale, for it bulges with unfiled reports and questionnaires needing answers, second and third class mail awaiting a glance, and intriguing documents deserving a more detailed examination. If people can climb the Alps, why can't I scale my pitiable peaks before they become insurmountable ranges snowcapped year 'round? I have the power to remove these mountains, don't I?

Ah, but love is my priority, according to Paul. It may seem that I am sidestepping the issue to suggest that, but really it's true. Love demands the institution of priorities, and needless mountaineering is not one of them. One has to pole vault innumerable academic problems, broad jump unaccountable personality issues, and run the race of teaching with such vigor in parish and school that desk Dolomites should be left to days when an athlete is no longer needed to wrestle that Pandora's box of troublesome conundrums to the ground. It's okay to put things aside, and no need to apologize for doing so.

How I wish I could hear that from another voice. How I yearn not to feel guilty for putting someone else's prime project on hold merely to attend to the important stuff, like living. So I wind up with both monumental mountain ranges atop and underneath my desk, while I discover another one pushing its way up from the bottom of the sea of tranquility within my psyche, unless I listen to Scripture. That's the time I need to realize that I don't possess all the supernatural powers necessary to deal with every mystery so that I can efficiently vaporize my desk-claiming mountain ranges with some imagined raygun. "Do not be anxious," says Jesus (Matthew 6:25). "Have no anxiety about anything," writes Paul (Philippians 4:6). What I have is a God who loves me, yes, me! In Christ, I am assured that his love is more important than leaping tall buildings and scaling the threatening volcanoes on top and beneath my desk. Did not Jesus insist to Martha that "One thing is needful (Luke 10:42)?" The care of the soul, including my soul, is more important than senseless guilt over Andean-like paperwork and Himalayan-tall promotional packets.

Take your E's with these three:

1. Evaluate essentials. These are the basics that must be done. Don't neglect prayer, or you won't get the rest of your work done, Luther once advised. But don't fail to work on your real work either, for no one else will do it. That's your calling.

2. Eliminate the unessentials. If you want to put them to the side for another day, good, but don't feel guilty about it. Work on love, even if you think you have all powers to do the

impossible. You emulate the Creator when you construct desktop mountains, but you're not an eternal God with limitless time to spend on unnecessary mountain climbing. He doesn't need to leave them for a future time as we do.

3. Enjoy loving and being loved in Christ, even while hating the realization that you're only human in your capacity to climb desk-top mountains.

George Mallory may have determined to climb mountains because they were there, but I like the idea of the American mathematician Edward Kasner, who delighted in organizing mountain-climbing expeditions to the highest point in Belgium. When asked how high that was, he would reply, "Twelve feet above sea level." You see, he had other priorities.

As Christian teachers, so do we. Let God lead you to master those and leave the unessential Mount Everests to someone used to rappeling up and down the top of the world.

Martin Luther

Schoolmaster

> *I charge you in the presence of God and of Christ Jesus who is to judge the living and the dead, and by his appearing and his kingdom: preach the word, be urgent in season and out of season, convince, rebuke, and exhort, be unfailing in patience and in teaching.*
> — *1 Timothy 4:1-2*

"No calling pleases me as well as that of schoolmaster; nor would I more gladly accept any other calling," said the reformer in 1530. He attested that "It takes persons of exceptional ability to teach and train children aright" in his encouragement of the establishment of public schools. For Luther, preaching and teaching the Word of God was fundamental to his existence.

A child was confused. He had just seen the latest *Superman* flick and heard one of the comic book hero's ardent foes addressed by a name that sounded like Luther. "I don't understand," he said to his second grade teacher, "If this Luther guy is so great here, why is he always out to get Superman? Isn't Superman a Christian, too?"

Similar-sounding names can confound the mature as well as the young, and the roles screen fantasies develop can make that complication even greater. Still Luther was not perfect. The Saxon professor blundered in his anti-Semitism, yet we remember him for teaching about the gospel to children, as well as princes and popes, peasants and other professionals. We can't excuse his excesses, but we can benefit from his experiences.

He was so given to teaching the Bible that he was like Jacob, we're told, wrestling with the living God and unwilling to give up until a blessing had been won. One of the reformer's opponents observed many years after having attended his classes, "The students heard him gladly, for they had never listened

15

to anyone like him, who so boldly translated every Latin word into German.'' He gave animation to the Word and thrills to those who heard it, so that they gasped in delight.

But it was not his own voice that made the classroom experience under Luther so fascinating. He was always well prepared with more notes than he could deliver. The students didn't suffer from a lack of information. In addition, he prepared synopses of passages he was discussing, which were printed for the use of the students atop the texts he had printed for distribution in the classroom. Copies of texts had wide margins, so the students could write their own notations along the edges. These were Luther's teaching innovations. He did everything he could to make learning the pleasure it needs to be.

For that reason, he counsels the rest of us by asking, ''What work is greater and more splendid than imparting real and true instruction? If, then, you are a teacher or the head of a school, what are you to do? You are faithfully to instruct, teach, discipline, and admonish the youth entrusted to you. You should do so expecting that some will do their duty and others will not. For he who wants to do good must expect that it is done in vain and that his good deed is poorly used, because the number of those who spurn good advice is always greater than the number of those who follow it. And we should be satisfied when the good we do has not been entirely lost. It is enough if one of the 10 lepers returns to acknowledge the benefit (Luke 17:17). So it is enough if one of 10 pupils takes correction and studies diligently; for thus the benefit is not altogether lost. And in imitation of the example which God gives us we are enjoined to do good to both the grateful and the ungrateful (Matthew 5:45).''

Luther was not Superman, but he did a super job in teaching us the wonder of God's grace and opening up to us the understanding that faith plays in accepting God's gift in Christ. In that, he continues to be a master educator today, challenging us to learn from his experience what he can to enable children to be more like the Christ we adore.

Hands That Help

Hand, *n. The terminal part of the arm when, as in man and some animals, it is specifically modified as a grasping organ. The hand includes the fingers and thumb, and the wrist.*

"See my hands and my feet, that it is I myself; handle me, and see; for a spirit has not flesh and bones as you see that I have.". — *Luke 24:39*

Jesus' hands are not described in Scripture. We don't know if they were large or small, rough or soft, bony or fleshy, but we do know they were generous, kindly, empowered. With a touch of his hand, the fever of Peter's mother-in-law disappeared (Matthew 8:15). With a reach of his hand, Peter himself was rescued from drowning (Matthew 14:31). A leper besought the Lord, "If you will, you can make me clean." With pity, Jesus "stretched out his hand and touched him, and said to him, 'I will; be clean' (Mark 1:40-41)." Jairus' daughter awakened from death as he took "her by the hand" and said, "Little girl, I say to you, arise (Mark 5:41)." Repeatedly, Jesus extended his hand.

It was so on the cross. His hands were riveted with nails, probably through the wrist, on that towering cross on Calvary, and there he offered his hands in total sacrifice. It was later Easter evening that he stood before the disciples in that upper gallery and displayed his hands, saying, "See my hands and my feet, that it is I myself; handle me, and see; for a spirit has not flesh and bones as you see that I have." Later, Thomas, who was not present, touched the very same hands in awe, and believed in his resurrection.

By a hand dipped in the bowl of food, Jesus identified his betrayer (Matthew 26:23). By his hand grasping a reed did the soldiers declare Jesus a king (Matthew 27:29). By a slapping hand, Jesus was punished by a soldier who reprimanded him before the high priest (John 18:22). It was with a gesture of his hand that our Lord identified his true mother and brothers (Matthew 12:46ff). It was by hyperbole that he told the sinful to cut off an offending hand or an errant foot, making it an example to squelch sin (Mark 9:43ff).

The hand in the Jesus story is never idle. When mothers brought their young children to Jesus for a blessing, he laid his hands up on them, despite the rebuke of the disciples for disturbing their master (Matthew 19:13-15). It was enough to make the incredulous people exclaim, "What mighty works are wrought by his hands (Mark 6:2)."

His were always helping hands.

In general imitation of him who is our Lord, teachers and aides touch their wards with commpassionate caring. In an era that can readily misinterpret a simple and sensible touch, those who teach dare not tie their hands behind their backs, because children need the warmth of a kindly hand. God has given us hands so that children may identify them as part of the geography of the teacher, and therefore sacred gifts. It's the teacher's hand that inscribes important ideas on the chalk-board. It's the teacher's hand that demonstrates a science lesson or trains them in art. It's a pointing hand that selects a participant, the finger to the lip that signals quiet, the hand waving that provides a warm greeting, and the artful signing of the hands that enables the deaf to hear.

Doris Pikop, the former directress of Our Saviour's Lutheran Church Preschool in Long Beach, California, spent long hours rubbing the backs of the toddlers in her charge to relax them and send them off to napping. Crouching beside them in a dimly-lit room as they lay on their cots, she and her aides made these moments tender times of communication for the wearied children. In an age that's caught on a speeding catapult, times like these become lasting memories. It's the hand that loves, as well as disciplines.

Lucy and Charlie Brown are at it eyeball to eyeball. Lucy holds up her hand and explains how each finger is different, richly unique, separate entities capable of a separate duties. These same five fingers, knotted together for a specific purpose, can become a unified fist and pack a wallop that could land Charlie Brown in the street, she reminds him. Looking at his own chubby fingers forlornly, Charlie Brown mutters, "Why can't you guys get together?"

In the geography of a teacher, we have hands that care, share and dare. We have hands that represent Jesus with a gentle touch, hands that work out problems on paper, make music on the piano, or deal with subjects on the computer. We are given hands to shake, hands to wring, hands to pat on the back, lower as well as upper. Hands can juggle balls as well as correct papers, open doors and lock windows. They can be nimble and quick taking roll, and slow and patient when they rest in the lap, but hands are always useful, because they don't belong to the teacher alone, but to Jesus.

One day, a raging drunk came into my office, swearing and belching, wildly haranguing, and belligerently sneering, and then with both fists he pounded on my desk with a tumultuous roar. A small statue of Thorvaldsen's Christus sitting on the edge of my desk, Come Unto Me, suddenly lost its arms, hands and all. They just fell off as if they had been cut. The drunk was shocked, and so was I. "Don't worry about it," I said quietly. "Now he has no hands but ours to do his will. But will you?"

The drunk had a sobering moment, but when I glued those hands and arms back on the figure of Jesus, I couldn't help wondering if it would have been better to leave them off. We are Jesus' hands. Let him hand it to you now: a new commandment to love one another, palms, wrists, fingers, thumbs and all.

David

Teaching Kings

And David said, "The Lord who delivered me from the paw of the lion and from the paw of the bear, will deliver me from the hand of this Philistine."
— *1 Samuel 17:37*

When but a toddler, Prince David (who later became King Edward VIII of Great Britain, and after his abdication, the Duke of Windsor) was dining with his grandfather, Edward VII. The small tyke had no fear of his grandfather and once interrupted his conversation during lunch with an anxious concern. The small prince was reprimanded and told to wait until given permission to speak. When his chance finally came, he spoke softly and unconcernedly. "It's too late now, grandpapa," he said while munching on a morsel. "It was a caterpillar on your lettuce, but you've eaten it."

The David of the Old Testament was not yet a prince, albeit someday he would be king. He, too, addressed a king out-of-turn. It should have been the generals and the colonels offering to defend Israel against the Philistine Goliath, but it was a shepherd boy who came, not only to save the nation, but to instruct King Saul in how to defeat an enemy. It was an audacious act, brazen and yet courageous far beyond that of the whole frightened army.

Loaded with the king's weighty armor, this young Bethlehemite was ready to be bargained to Goliath and defeat if he allowed himself to be dragged to the battlefield dressed like a junkyard nightmare. After all, King Saul stood head and shoulders above everyone else, which meant little David literally was drowning in all that bronze. Having fought off the marauding lions and bears eager to lunch on his father's flocks without the benefit of breastplates and shields, young David was not about to submit to the defeat such armor provided. All he needed were pebbles for his sling and the maneuverability of a shepherd protecting his sheep. He was the athlete ready to wrestle a tyrant rather than unwary prey ready to submit to defeat. He told the king, and the king listened.

King Edward VII should have learned from Saul to pay attention to underage subjects also.

Many an instructor is the monarch in the classroom. The Davids among the boys and girls enrolled need not wear their teacher's protective gear to battle academic and social threats. All they need is what David had: faith and a few pebbles for their slingshot.

One pebble is the will to say no. Children and adults equipped with fanciful programs may be like an armor-clad David, when all they need to know is how to spurn wrong by saying a forceful "no," whether to drugs, sexual advances, or other ills. The Commandments provide a ready guide.

A second pebble is the one that says yes to healthy opportunities. David had no fear of Goliath, because he had said yes to God. Teachers and their charges do well to practice affirming the faith they believe in concrete, observable ways. The Apostles' Creed is a worthy companion.

Another rock is the assurance that Jesus is Lord. In appointing Peter to be the rock upon whose witness the church would be built, Jesus was singling out the importance of an unwavering faith. David championed the messianic promise, a small pebble of great importance. The sacraments are pebbles to be kept in every young David's spiritual wallet.

Out of the desert gravel, a fourth pebble to be taken along should be one of courage. Goliath stood 10 feet six, and would have been better playing basketball for the Phoenix Suns that attacking Israel. David packed along a grain of courage that was big enough to conquer the threat if he would not wear the king's armor. He knew the promises of the Scriptures. It's a word to be related to every experience.

And lastly, take along the pebble of truth. David, stripped bare of the coat of mail and the bronze helmet, had God's Word to encourage him. Truth and a slingshot can go a long way in defeating the belligerents in life today, wherever the

battlefield. A faith developed is truth expressed, like
cleansed of its earthy covering.

Sometimes it pays to interrupt the noble. Edward
have avoided that extra bit of protein had he list
princely grandson. Fortunately, King Saul paid attention. Un-
fortunately, Goliath did not.

Equip yourself with your shepherd's bag of smooth pebbles from the brook of hope, walk with your staff determined,
and humble today's Goliaths gladly.

Deserts Of Failure?

Desert, *n. An arid region lacking moisture to support vegetation.*

. . . They were stoned, they were sawn in two, they were killed with the sword; they went about in skins of sheep and goats, destitute, afflicted, ill-treated — of whom the world was not worthy — wandering over deserts and mountains, and in dens and caves of the earth.
— *Hebrews 11:37-39*

It is a paragraph filled with the anguish of the martyrs of ancient times. We hear of wastelands that literally wasted men and women, extravagantly pouring these riches, like refuse, into the abyss of failure. They were prophets and teachers, the simple and the sophisticated, the pious and the proud, but they were people God used. It was not their failure, however, but that of those who abused them.

Deserts are among the most successful living laboratories on earth. The animal and plant life that dwell there master the extremes of severe nightly cold and blistering, burning daytime heat, not to mention their bleak economy of food and water. They know how to store moisture, to drink it out of the air and pour it upon their parched roots, these plant survivors of the desert. The slithering denizens of the desert are well aware of these sources of much-needed drink. The desert is one of God's great marvels, a success that most would think totally impossible.

Benjamin Barber, an eastern university professor, says, "I don't divide the world into the weak and the strong, or the successes and the failures, those who make it or those who don't. I don't even divide the world into the extroverted and the introverted, or those who hear the inner voice or the outer voice, because we all hear some of both. I divide the world," he reveals, "into learners and nonlearners."

25

So it is that we endure the deserts through which we must sometimes roam. We Christians go not as failures, but those equipped to succeed, to learn and unlearn, but we are never to be nonlearners. The Israelites spent 40 years wandering the baldest deserts of the world in search of the land of promise. While it was not all pleasant, they were not without success. John the Baptist made that hostile and desolate environment a place to succeed also, not just survive. Jesus, in the bitterness of the Devil's evil temptations, demonstrated that no one need yield to the harsh rigors deserts evoke if he or she is willing to dredge up the memory of God and his Word, living like the desert itself, needing little from without, yet feasting on what's within. Is this not what his fasting in the wilderness teaches us?

How prisoners endured merciless treatment in the cages of the Viet Cong is one of this era's impressive tales. Many steeled themselves from madness by reflecting on memories lodged deep inside, calling upon an inner strength to cope with outer insanity. They are among history's most heroic learners. For some it was home life they remembered, the joys of the family, the beauty of holiday closeness, while for others it was Scripture passages of hope and assurance and encouragement. Natan Sharansky, the Russian Jewish dissident, survived the brutality of his treatment at the hands of the Soviet KGB by improving and sharpening his Hebrew vocabulary, and, although tone deaf, singing meaningful lyrics! Katherine Kuhlman managed her captivity by the Iranian radicals after the capture of the American Embassy with the singing of hymns and the richness of prayer. Corrie ten Boom and her sister got through the ordeal of a concentration camp sharing snips of Bible verses and joining in on the serenity of Christian prayer. Deserts are not to waste their travelers just because they are wastelands themselves. It's a classroom for learning.

The struggle in the inner city is said to be like contending with a famine on a desert island surrounded by an impenetrable glass vial with a river of fresh water and banks of resplendent fruitful fields on the other side. One either develops the mentality of the gila monster and the saquaro cactus or fails, longing for the lush greenness beyond. We need to be learners. The strength must come from within, as it did for Gideon, Barak, Samson, Jephthah, David and Samuel about whom the writer to the Hebrews speaks.

The gila monster doesn't think about what it doesn't have. It does not surrender to jealousy or give in to despair. It creatively deals with what is readily available, and thrives! John ate wild honey and locusts in the wilderness and evidently prospered. After all, he had a coterie of disciples, who would not have followed had his been merely a gaunt existence without any provisions. Survivors must weigh the value of every possibility, which is precisely what the administrator in Christian schools must do. If found in the midst of a mean and arid desert, that inventory has to be inclusive of every life-sustaining potential.

When my children were younger and we lived on the desert, we did not have far to walk to reach vast undeveloped expanses. "I don't know why cactus has to have thorns," said Jenny one day. "With all this room, who would want to sit on it anyway?" But if you're thirsty, that's the place to find liquid to refresh a parched tongue. No wonder the cactus has spines, it defends the desert's most treasured resource with its own effective security system.

Christian schools, like prickly pear cactus, need to protect their resources for the very purpose of allowing wanderers in sin's desert to drink of the goodness stored up inside.

Deserts are environments that can teach us a great deal about life and witness, surviving and caring. They teach us how to be learners in God's garden, rather than failures in the deserts of human difficulty.

Johann Sebastian Bach

Choirmaster

> *Sing to the Lord a new song, his praise from the end of the earth! Let the sea roar and all that fills it, the coastlands and their inhabitants. Let the desert and its cities lift up their voice, the villages that Kedar inhabits; let the inhabitants of Sela sing for joy, let them shout from the top of the mountains. Let them give glory to the Lord . . .*
> — *Isaiah 42:10-12a*

He had the incredible ability to stick it out. It could be nothing other than a divine calling. And it was. Johann Sebastian Bach was cantor of the Thomas Church in Leipzig for 27 years. During that time, he experienced the attitude of the town council, and the impudence of disrespectful students, personal deserts that did not deter his praise of a magnificent God. He was paid a good deal less than was possible as a court musician and forced to teach academic as well as musical subjects in the school, including catechism, coordinate the music for five of Leipzig's' churches, prepare special motets, oratorios, and other works for the customary four-hour services on Sunday, conduct choirs, serve as organist for weddings and funerals, give singing lessons, and shuffle innumerable papers, and still he could praise God with an unfathomable joy.

He stuck it out.

They cut his salary because he did not always handle the details of his duties as faithfully as he prepared the wondrous music of his compositions and accomplished the rest of his music ministry. They were blind, these naysayers, to Bach's worth, men of narrowed minds. Yet Bach offered God exultant praise.

Bach was there to serve God. It was God who called him. And it was God who was heard in the soaring tones and impressive words of his cantatas. Said the non-Christian philosopher Friedrich Nietzsche, after hearing Bach's *St. Matthew*

Passion in 1870, "One who has completely forgotten Christianity truly hears it here as Gospel."

As teachers, we can cave in to demands that exceed our capacities or to complaints that ignore our greater accomplishments, or to salary cuts or raises that don't match secular possibilities, but to make music like Bach, all we need to hear is God calling us to a task that he wants us to fulfill. Then our teaching praises him. Isn't this the witness the cantor of Leipzig offers us yet? It's not "poor me," but "Praise God!"

His housing conditions were miserable. His children suffered because of it, as did his wife. Bach worked all the harder to improve his lot. Still the music poured like an everlasting waterfall from his heart to those who abused him, hopeful that somehow they would hear the goodness of Christ and live accordingly. Many did, but the town fathers, who had control of the churches' schools and music programs, did not. They demanded that he prepare cantatas for secular festival days no fewer than 53 times during his tenure in Leipzig, above and beyond his already demanding load, and he did it!

Small-minded souls exist and the only way to stretch their capacity is not to give up, but to reach inside their souls and expand their limitations with the power of a thousand angels singing God's praises. That's what Bach did and continues to do, and what teachers who hear God's call are capable of doing today. It is not that they should remain squeakless doormats, but sing God's praises so loudly and well that even those with musical impediments catch the spirit.

At the beginning of his works, Bach would often inscribe "In Jesus' name," at the conclusion, "To God alone the glory," which may account for the reason he never sought to publish his compositions. They were gifts to God, and so must be the music of every Christian teacher, bits of praise that honor God, enrich the teacher's soul, and inspire struggling students, too, and whatever town council to whom they pay their respects.

Eyes That See Beyond

Eye, *n. The organ of sight; esp. the nearly spherical mass, the eyeball, in a bony concavity of the skull; the faculty of seeing; vision.*

And as Jesus passed on from there, two blind men followed him, crying aloud, "Have mercy on us, Son of David." When he entered the house, the blind men came to him; and Jesus said to them, "Do you believe that I am able to do this?" They said to him, "Yes, Lord." Then he touched their eyes, saying, "According to your faith be it done to you." And their eyes were opened.
— Matthew 9:27-30

Microscopes can probe the smallest mysteries. Telescopes can plumb the depths of outer space. But only God can see beyond the present moment. We can look into the past, digging deep into the ruins of bygone civilizations and personal problems, or we can project potential needs and environmental difficulties far into the future for humanity in general and ourselves specifically, but no one except the triune God sees the inner needs of humanity collectively, and you and me precisely, past, present, or future.

God, however, gives us clues about the future. Jesus spelled out a number of "signs in sun and moon and stars" to look for, as he enjoined the Twelve to be ready: "Now when these things begin to take place, look up and raise your heads, because your redemption is drawing near (Luke 21:25-28)." But the faithful teacher must not wait until some future time to ready the embryonic class for Christ's coming. Nor should any teacher put off being prepared for a flurry of problems now. Developing the vision that sees beyond requires a rare sensitivity.

Henry van Dyke writes of such a man in his poem *The Toiling of Felix*, a man who yearned to envision Christ. He attempted the discipline of silence, "keeping vigil night and day" in the "shrines where Christians come to pray." He found a saintly hermit, and though he could not provide an answer to the urgent quest, the desert wanderer gave him a worn bit of papyrus with these words illuminated upon it in gilded hues, "Raise the stone, and thou shalt find me, cleave the word, and there am I." Finally, Felix went back to work, his venture over. He labored in a rock quarry, hewing stone, aiding his fellow workers in their struggles, and praying at last, "Though I see thee not, I love thee. Let me do thy humblest task!" In that willingness came his vision. "Can it be," Felix wondered, "that men must seek him at their toil 'mid rocks and trees?"

That's where blind eyes are. To search only for the Damascus Road experience is to become blind like Paul to the Christ who is ever present. It is when we commit ourselves to serving him in our daily tasks, our mundane routines, our simple expressions and least formal thoughts and associations, as well as the grand ventures, that we find him and we see with clarity.

When Linda DeHart was beginning a section on baptism in her third grade class, it was a commonplace study, similar to that in many Christian schools, but something happened in the process. Christ was there. The Holy Spirit was nudging souls and touching hearts. Twelve students sought to be baptized, most of them in her class, yet some were in other classes, who heard the students share their joy in discovering the wonder of the sacrament. There were two sets of twins. Somehow, they saw Jesus, not like trees walking (Mark 8:24), but with clarity of vision. The Word had been shared and the invitation personally felt. Like Felix, they had their vision of the Christ who cares discovered virtually in cleaving wood and lifting stone.

Erma Bombeck wrote *Aunt Erma's Cope Book* after reading 62 books and articles on self-help. She did all the self-analyzing, introspective things advised and came to grips with midlife, inner peace, and her deepest fantasies. She even fought outer flab, examined her motives for buying, dissected her marriage, and tried every technique urged, but all that happened was that she got tired of herself. There was no vision, no seeing beyond the immediate moment.

She wrote, "I used to wallow — no, nearly drown — in wonderful funky days of despair when nothing went right, and I loved it. Those down-in-the-dirty-pits days when I was unappreciated, overworked, underpaid, and had split heels from not wearing socks in the winter." But then, she concluded, the only "how-to" book she had the expertise to write was one she called *How to Get from Monday to Friday in Twelve Days*. There, in the actual grind, is where vision comes to refresh the soul and enable us to face another day. It is having blind eyes healed and sight restored to see plainly, as Felix found, underneath the raised stone and the cleaved timber is God knitting together the separated strands of the personality and life to make a fabric of gladness.

Ridding oneself of sin's taint through renewal of the baptismal covenant is opening the eyes to see with his vision a future that's filled with opportunity and grace. We have this geography in him: eyes that see beyond.

Moses

The Family That Teaches Together Learns

And when she could hide him no longer she took for him a basket made of bulrushes and daubed it with bitumen and pitch; and she put the child in it and placed it among the reeds at the river's brink. And his sister stood at a distance, to know what would be done to him.
— *Exodus 2:3-4*

It was no great academic institution, but what a faculty!

A mother demonstrated cleverness as the administrator of the family's educational system. The older sister was an adjunct professor of caring, until the mother regained her role as dean of faith and enlisted a princess to become a visiting professor of Egyptian culture while also supplying the endowment to success. In fact, Dean Jochebed virtually hired Pharaoh and his whole palace staff to teach Moses how to survive in that inhospitable land's threatening environment. We learn that the family that teaches together not only learns, but earns surprising joys.

Leave it to Jochebed to jockey around the proscriptions of Egypt's king. And leave it to Miriam to transform a dangerous liaison into a profitable arrangement. Imagine not only rescuing a baby brother's life, but getting someone else to fund his existence, too. Here is the quality of creativity (what the Jews call *chutzpah*) required by Christian schools to master deficits and spark scholarships. First, one must see that threats are dangers to be challenged.

Begin with a little boat. Jochebed did not attempt to construct Noah's ark or build the prototype for Cunard's QE 2. She had a smaller vessel in mind. She wove a basket of bulrushes and made it watertight with bitumen and pitch. She took a huge idea and worked it out in its smallness so completely that it would not only float, but little Moses would be safe. It was a gigantic idea sized for the situation. It was as if she had been living Paul Laurence Dunbar's 'words, which I have altered to fit Jochebed's role:

She labored hard and failed at last,
Her sails too weak to bear the blast,
The raging tempests tore away
And sent her beating bark astray.
   But what cared she
   For wind or sea!
She said, "The tempest will be short,
My bark will come to port."
She saw through every cloud a gleam —
   She had her dream.

A messiah was the Father's dream also, a little babe with tiny arms and wondering eyes, a child as vulnerable as Moses, and with his own boat of reeds fashioned into a stable manger. Ironically, Joseph and Mary would flee with Jesus to Egypt for safety, even as Moses would lead the Israelites in a reverse journey to the safety of the Land of Promise. Yet both families, the one by the Nile and the other not far from the Jordan, would see enormous hopes, the colossal ideas of faith, become the means by which God would reorder his world.

Begin with an idea, a fragile, but seaworthy craft, and let it float, keeping a watchful eye. Then enlist the whole family in your quest for security and discover princesses and pharaohs acquiescing to your hopes. Who can let a good idea die, or a child sail aimlessly about and miss a broadened education? You will find the simple weaving together of thoughts out of plain experience is as radical a concept as rocketing to the planets. The family is a faculty all its own, and yet one that needs to become a branch to those who find the classroom their laboratory.

Patrick Henry, one of the greatest orators America ever produced, and the only governor to serve five terms, had a mother like Jochebed. She made everyone an assistant professor in her son's upbringing, especially the clergy. One of her customs was to require young Pat to take copious notes of every sermon, and she took him to hear every great preacher who came to town. Then he had to repeat the sermons to her on return trips from church with every inflection. He learned the Bible and oratory at the same time, becoming the greatest spellbinder of the time, as well as the most activist attorney in the colonies on religious freedom issues. Like Israel with Moses, this nation was the richer for Mrs. Henry making the family a university worthy of enrollment.

Seas Of Delight

Sea, *n. One of the larger bodies of salt water, less than an ocean. An ocean.*

The earth is the Lord's and the fullness thereof, the world and those who dwell therein; for he has founded it upon the seas, and established it upon the rivers.
— *Psalm 24:1-2*

When my son Deryk was small, he used to sing "Onward Christian Soldiers," *standing on the shore.* I was never quite sure if he was unwilling to push off into spiritual warfare, or merely mishearing the lyric. I presumed the latter. But too often we Christian educators are singing those words ourselves.

Spiritual joy, dynamic lesson plans, a team of dedicated co-laborers in support families, and our colleagues fuel us with the essential energy to vault the separating seas like soaring rockets to pioneer new ventures far beyond the safety of our own tranquil harbors. Yet, all too often, we are content to be "standing on the shore."

"The earth is the Lord's," we agree, and we'll keep to *terra firma,* lest we drown while swimming to another beach, we say in defense of our timidity. But, sings the psalmist, "He founded it upon the seas, and established it upon the rivers." God created those, too! We have not only the right to explore, but the encouragement to sail beyond the shallow water of our home port across the spiritual seas to apply the truths we teach on our own familiar shores. We may not want to march off to war, but how about "launching out to roar?"

Let it roar. Take notice of a world out there yearning for discovery! Your sea may be no wider than your street or no further across than across the block. There are children and adults and whole families, who could benefit from a sustained involvement with you, not a quick fix, a hasty lunar-landing with a rapid return intended only for the 11 o'clock news. Push off in canoes or kayaks, cruise ships or speedboats, alone or with a crew, but sail to discover a long-term mission you can germinate.

Let it roar some more. Develop a free after-school tutoring program for the neighbor kids not enrolled in your school. See how you can enrich their lives and the community, and take away the stigma of being an institution only for the well-to-do or the parish elite.

Let it roar around the world! Imaginative teachers and inspired students, together with creative board members, supporting families, and eager congregations, can discover a new world close at hand or far off, one that meets the challenge of Christian soldiers no longer being left standing on the shore. Be a Columbus to prove the world is round, that we care about the "other side" as we do our own.

St. Timothy's in San Jose has a weekly program that brings in wheelchair youngsters from a nearby government-operated institution to establish relationships and provide friendships. Both the handicapped and the school benefit, and the love of Christ becomes ocean deep, and a merry sea of delight.

Robert Fulghum gained a bestseller by telling us *All I Really Need to Know I Learned in Kindergarten* in his 1988 book. (Share everything, play fair, don't hit people, put things back where you found them, and so forth). Christians can paraphrase his title by saying all we really need to know is what we learned in John 3:16: "For God so loved the world that he gave his only son, that whoever believes in him should not perish but have eternal life." (Let God love you, believe in him, share his goodness.) That does not mean standing on the shore.

Onward, then, Christian soldiers. There are seas to cross and oceans of joy awaiting us.

Raoul Wallenberg

An Example For Everyone

> *Greater love has no man than this, that a man lay down his life for his friends.* John 15:13

Luther had his classroom lectern. Bach possessed a choirloft podium. Teachers customarily have a rostrum from which to lecture, or a chalkboard on which to diagram, or a laboratory table from which to demonstrate. But Raoul Wallenberg had neither school nor church from which to teach the lessons he had to instruct carefully. He had, instead, the aching, tormented city of Budapest, its train stations and ghettos, collecting points for yellow star-wearing Jewish detainees, synagogues, hospitals, and orphanages.

Wallenberg was a Lutheran, who, during his college years at the University of Michigan, attended worship services with a young lady named Bernice Ringman, who related these facts to me. In his native Sweden, he was baptized and confirmed and sang in church choirs and participated in Handel's oratorios. Then he became a banker in South Africa and Haifa before returning to his homeland to a life as a businessman. He was involved in importation and exportation throughout Europe, but mainly in Hungary. Later on, when World War II raged feverishly throughout Europe, and neutral Sweden's king was asked by President Franklin Roosevelt to provide an envoy to rescue the remaining Jews in Nazi-dominated Hungary, Raoul Wallenberg was chosen.

He was undaunted in his determination to save the Jews from the concentration camps. Budapest housed the last large remaining Jewish population. Already, Eichmann had rounded up the Jews in the provinces and elsewhere throughout the Nazi-controlled areas, so that only the Jews of Budapest remained. They, too, were herded into boxcars and marched to the gas chambers. Wallenberg, however, defied the swastika-wearing enemies, claiming many of the Jews being rounded up

41

were eligible for Swedish passports. He invented a special, albeit illegal, passport to distribute, and saved many because of it. Since it looked official, the Nazis presumed it was. He told elderly Jews, "I'm sorry, but I have come to save a nation. I must save the young ones first." It was a bitter "Sophie's Choice" he had to make, but in the end, because of his heroism, he rescued by himself or with the aid of other diplomats at least 120,000 Jews. Among them today are a U.S. congressman and his wife, as well as concert artists, scientists, and prominent leaders in other nations, and many an average citizen.

What he taught was that love knows no limits. Paul had written, "Love bears all things, believes all things, hopes all things, endures all things. Love never ends (1 Corinthians 13:7-8a)." Jesus had taught his followers the audacious concept to love both their neighbors and their enemies. Wallenberg knew these were more than nice-sounding phrases, but pragmatic directions to living the Christian faith. Despite some biographies denying Wallenberg's Christian beliefs, Miss Ringman said differently. A learned rabbi at the Los Angeles Wiesenthal Center could only attribute his heroism to the Christianity with which he grew up. The example was too clearly that of a man of conviction to be any different, he said.

Translated into our present circumstance, to teach like Wallenberg means to let love refuse every destructive barrier. We cannot subscribe to the gospel and ignore responsibilities to confront boldly sin and error. It happens on the playground and in the lunchroom, at staff meetings and congregational events. Winsome as that young Swede, face up to unpopular duties and rescue the slandered from abuse, the innocent from the hateful, and the eager from the ignorant. You may not have to lay down your life, but merely to lay down your convictions is not enough either.

Wallenberg's story doesn't end with the heroics of Budapest. He is the last remaining victim still immersed in the bitter consequences of the Holocaust. For more than 40 years he has been an unwilling captive of the Soviet Union.

His last sighting was in 1987. No one ever said that all heroics will be adequately rewarded, but that is no reason for not living Christ's admonition to love. None whatsoever.

Putting Your Foot Down

> **Foot,** *n. The terminal part of the leg; that part of an animal upon which it rests when standing, or upon which it moves.*

> *Stand therefore . . .*   — *Ephesians 6:14*

My granddaughter Erin, edging toward three, was standing in my living room after the 400-mile drive from Phoenix, looking cute and cuddly.

"Come on over," I beckoned in my most grandfatherly tone.

Suddenly, she screwed up her face in a scowl, stomped her bare right foot thunderously and bellowed, "No!"

She had definitely put her foot down. For some reason, I felt as though she was mimicking someone else rather than responding to my paternal call. Later on that same day, I saw her mother, my daughter, use precisely the same technique in preventing Erin from exploiting the "terrifying twos" any further. Down came the right foot, and out trumpeted a decisive negative exclamation: No! Kristyn had put her foot down emphatically, and Erin responded immediately.

There comes a time for taking a stand. It's always well to evaluate whether putting one's foot down is a matter of lording a personal whim or employing the Lord's will. It could be putting an unappetizing foot into one's mouth to become totalitarian. I've discovered I have little room for one there, let alone both monstrous hooves. It's not only difficult to apologize, but impossible to eat.

Paul says that taking a stand is possible when one is equipped to do so. God arms us with loins girded with truth, dressing us with the breastplate of righteousness, and shoes that possess the equipment of the gospel of peace, while providing us with faith's shield, salvation's helmet, and the Spirit's sword, which is the word of God. With these assets, we can take a stand that is well-grounded (Ephesians 5:10ff). We seek to be strong in the Lord, not merely mighty in ourselves, garbed in the whole armor he shares, rather than vulnerable to devilish attack.

But putting our foot down should mean also we stroll "the paths of righteousness for his name's sake (Psalm 23:3)." It is then we wipe the Lord's feet with both our tears and hair, as did the repentent women in Simon's house, and anoint them with the ointment of love (Luke 7:36ff).

For that reason, we do well to sing with the children:

> *Little feet be careful*
> *Where you take me to.*
> *Anywhere for Jesus*
> *Only let me do.*

Our feet must be his feet, the "feet of him who brings good tidings of good, who publishes salvation, who says to Zion, 'Your God reigns.' (Isaiah 52:7). Our feet are his to enter into lives and homes, classrooms and playgrounds to share his joy. That's putting one's foot down, not with thunder, but a symphony of satisfaction.

When Jesus was ubraided for not preventing the woman from rinsing his feet with her tears, Jesus reminded his host, "I entered your house, you gave me no water for my feet, but she has wet my feet with her tears and wiped them with her hair. You gave me no kiss, but from the time I came in she has not ceased to kiss my feet. You did not anoint my head with oil, but she has anointed my feet with ointment. Therefore I tell you, her sins, which are many, are forgiven, for she loved much; but he who is forgiven little, loves little."

To love more, walk in her steps. To love even more than that, step into his sandals. It is when you wear his shoes that you see not only how much bigger he is, but how much you can continue to grow to fill them.

If you need to put your foot down, be sure that you can also get off on the right foot afterward as you start life anew.

A mother, deeply upset, wrote the principal a stinging rebuke. She had observed a Christian school preparing for Halloween. They had decorated with the typical black cats, witches and broomsticks, skulls and skeletons, jack-o-lanterns and ghosts, which in her mind enunciated pagan superstitions. Children were to dress up in costumes, and that angered her more. She put her foot down, but it was discovered, as the principal and the staff put their feet into Jesus' shoes, there are positive ways to walk lovingly with criticism, correct errors, and still recognize the event, decorating appropriately, and having Christian fun without giving mixed signals.

The geography of the teacher includes feet, despite their size, that can take a stand without tripping over one another in the process and walk all the way to learning the needful lesson.

Peter

Keeping At It!

"But Peter continued knocking . . .   — Acts 12:16

Andrew had fallen in love. He was only four, and Kathy was six, but he was smitten. He chased her around the large assembly room the day care program utilized and tried to convince Kathy he was serious. She preferred jumping rope and playing with her peers. Finally, in desperation, Andrew jumped on Kathy and started choking her.

"Now will you marry me?" he demanded.

"No," she screamed, "I'd rather die."

What Andrew's technique lacked, his persistence enlisted. He kept on even though it wasn't getting him anywhere. Kathy wasn't at all interested. It was just the opposite in the home of John Mark. The maid Rhoda was exceptionally interested in the voice heard on the other side of the door. It was Peter. He had been locked up in a Jerusalem jail cell at the order of Herod, who, as Luke says, was laying "violent hands" upon the church's leaders. Rhoda was so surprised to have him free that she ran to tell the others that he was there, leaving him at the unopened gate.

"You are mad," harangued the residents.

"But Peter continued knocking," reports Luke.

The door was finally opened as a reward to his persistence. With a little kindlier attention, Kathy might have acquiesced to Andrew's charms. He needed to keep knocking instead of choking. When one considers all kinds of ways Peter could have gotten their attention, screaming and yelling, banging and pounding, setting fire to the door, enlisting a Roman catapult, we need to honor his calm, caring persistence. He just kept knocking.

That may seem insufficient to getting the attention necessary in a youngster or a parent or colleague on the staff, but continued knocking will inevitably get the necessary attention in a far more suitable way than causing an uproar.

Peter must have learned his patience from Jesus. Does not the Lord say, "Behold, I stand at the door and knock; if any one hears my voice and opens the door, I will come in to him and eat with him, and he with me (Revelations 3:20)"? How often he knocks, and how frequently we, like Rhoda, go running in the opposite direction, knowing what we've heard, but unwilling to quiet our surprises long enough to let him in!

He's knocking now, like Peter, with quiet determination. He wants to enter your life this day, to fill it with promise.

Andrew will learn that one day. Perhaps another Kathy will benefit from his new-found wisdom.

It took this nation less than a decade to finally boost off to the moon. The Curies spent endless months looking for radium. Edison could not find the right filament for his incandescent lamp right away either. Jonas Salk bruised the door knocking for long years seeking a polio cure, just as AIDS researchers must do now. One day cancer will know its cure, just as scarlet fever and measles already have. But one must continue to knock.

Let the world know you exist and that you can implant the joy of Christianity into the heart of sobering math and complicated science, history's many-faceted truths, and art's deepest pleasures. Keep knocking. Jesus does.

Moving Off The Plateau

Plateau, n. An elevated tract of land; a tableland; similar to a mesa, a flat-topped rocky hill with steeply sloping sides, common in southwestern U.S.

I say to you, if you have faith as a grain of mustard seed, you will say to this mountain, "Move hence to yonder place," and it will move; and nothing will be impossible to you.
— *Matthew 17:20-21*

William L. Shirer, author of the classic *Rise and Fall of the Third Reich*, at 82 was preparing one volume of his memoirs for television, developing a play intended for Broadway, and taking lessons in Russian. He says all of this he was doing "just to get the cobwebs out of my brain." It was his way of moving off the plateau, reaching out to a new challenge, and sharpening his senses for the world before him.

It doesn't take much for Christians to get going again, to ease off the plateau and soar into ecstatic new heights! Jesus says a grain of faith is all that's needed, one no bigger than a mustard seed.

Johannes Brahms determined to stop composing. Whatever years were left to him, he wanted to enjoy, so he told everyone that he had quit writing music. A few months passed, but eventually, without much effort, he found himself writing once more, the notes fairly flying from his pen to the paper.

"I thought you weren't going to write any more," needled a friend.

"I wasn't," was the retort, "but after a few days away from it, I was so happy at the thought of no more writing that the music came to me without effort."

My view of Mount Nebo, where Moses delighted in the panoramic spectacular of the promised land in its entirety, is that it appears to be a mountain from the western approach

51

only. From the east, the rise is so gentle that those traveling there feel they are more on a lofty plateau, a broad-backed mesa, a rising tableland, rather than a towering peak. Both times I have been atop Mount Nebo, I have been surprised by the differences in the two approaches: the westernmost part of the mountain is an edge that drops off almost 4,000 feet to the area of the Dead Sea. It is a sudden and severe plunge, in direct contrast to the eastward slope, a rugged mountain tableland, not at all fearsome. It's an unfrightening wilderness there, stark but comparatively tame.

Joshua, who had more than one grain of faith for conquering Canaan, pushed off from that seeming plateau to the new challenges in the land Abraham settled. Moses was left behind. There are times in our own lives when we need to let the Moses within us remain on the mountaintop, while we take sail, like a Joshua, eager to achieve God's grand design, ascending from the plateau only to descend to a promised land. But who dares jump from a 4,000-foot high summit?

A glider might. A skydiver with a trusty parachute could. And someone with a grain of mustard seed-sized faith who seeks to remove the mountain. Sometimes the reason we're stuck on a plateau is because the plateau is one we've conjured up in our minds. Removing that mountain will put you on ground level in nothing flat! It can send you into conquering a land of promise. Jesus says we can handle mountains, the mesas that seem so immovable, that way. "Move hence to yonder place," we are to say, and discover it moves. In fact, it disappears!

What is the plateau that's holding you back from lifting off to new opportunities? It may be yourself giving you a mountain of difficulty, as it was for Brahms.

It doesn't seem that William Shirer is left stranded on a mesa, does it? But he was once canned from a job, and it was a year or so before an opportunity came his way. He was on a plateau that didn't seem to budge. But it did. He's been dusting out the cobwebs of his mind ever since.

In Christ, we have one who knows how to deal with mountains. In the wilderness after his baptism, Jesus was tempted by Satan. The King James Version says that the devil took "him up into a high mountain," where he showed him all the nations of the earth (Luke 4:5). Jesus was not mastered by the devil's blandishments. Again, on the Mount of Transfiguration, Jesus demonstrated another mastery of the mesa as the voice of God assured the disciples with Jesus he was indeed a towering bridge to certainty (Matthew 17:1ff). But it was Calvary that Jesus disintegrated with his faith. It was more than planting a mustard seed, but you and I, well aware of his struggle in the Garden of Gethsemane, can see he mastered the plateau by challenging the mountain. No longer was he begging for the cup to be removed (Matthew 26:39). Now it was, "It is finished (John 19:30)." That begins for us when we stop saying "I can't" and begin asserting "God can!" "All things are possible to he who believes (Mark 9:23)," said Jesus, who likewise said "nothing will be impossible to you" when you sow the mustard seed of faith.

Take a grain of faith, prescribes Jesus, and I'll call you in the morning to leap into a new excitement that will thrill you and many.

Archbishop Desmond Tutu

A Happy Voice For Sad Situations

> *In those days came John the Baptist, preaching in the wilderness of Judea, "Repent, for the kingdom of heaven is at hand." For this is he who was spoken of by the prophet Isaiah when he said, "The voice of one crying in the wilderness: Prepare the way of the Lord, make his paths straight."*
> — *Matthew 3:1-3*

John the Baptist seems a dour prophet when set alongside Desmond Tutu, who, though engaged in the most serious problems of a troubled state, manages always to find a glimmer of humor. It's the teacher's tactic, the capability of discovering a pleasant lesson in an unpleasant situation, of finding joy amidst the chaos of inhuman actions.

A *tutu* is a dancer's dress, silly," announced a six-year-old, "not a archdishup!" She was correcting an older sibling who had just seen Archbishop Tutu in a television news program, and was explaining to a parent something the South African cleric had said. If there is anything that Desmond Tutu is not, it is a frilly skirt, but he does "dish up" a great deal to provoke thought and inspire sane, solid action, and he does it with wondrous Christian joy.

Born in Klerksdorp, a community in the Western Transvaal, October 7, 1931, to a Methodist schoolteacher, young Desmond received his education in a Swedish Lutheran boarding school at Roodeport. At age 14, stricken with tuberculosis, the lad spent nearly two years in a Sophiatown hospital sponsored by the fathers of the Community of the Resurrection, an Anglican order. There he came in contact with Trevor Huddleston, later Bishop of Mauritius, who visited him weekly in the hospital. They became fast friends, and the influence Huddleston had continued to flower in Tutu's life, even to Desmond naming one of his sons after the Anglican prelate.

He did not choose to become a clergyman immediately. In fact, he trained as a teacher in Pretoria and taught school for four years in Johannesburg and Krugersdorp, where he married Leah, a former pupil of his father, and also a teacher. It was while he was teaching in an American seminary in 1984 that he learned he was the recipient of the Nobel Peace Prize for that year. Then and there, he led his students in a merry dance of jubilation. A great deal happened between his becoming an Anglican priest and the Nobel Prize laureate, but in all of it one can see clearly the marks of the teacher carefully crafting his class from one stage of thought to another, until early into the 1990s South Africa will be ready to abandon *apartheid* and opt for a more open society.

To name Steve Biko, Robert Sobukwe, Winnie and Nelson Mandela, Alan Boesak, and Desmond Tutu is to list a pantheon of stalwart proponents of change. Alan Paton, the white author, told the story of that struggle between the patient and the impatient South Africans in his best-selling novels *(Cry the Beloved Country, Too Late the Phalarope, Ah, But Your Land is Beautiful)*. It is the cry of that voice in the wilderness again, of John the Baptist pointing toward Jesus, teaching the crowds to repent and prepare for the kingdom Christ brings. It is done, however, with such joy, such vitality, such hope, that one welcomes the sparkle Desmond Tutu brings to the glowering scene of human abuse. John Webster says one of the gleaming gifts Tutu brings to the South Africa that is his classroom, is "the emphasis he places on human power and potential. So many are repelled by a view of humanity that seems joyless and depressing, and it is remarkable that though Tutu works in a situation where *apartheid* reveals the selfish and destructive aspects of humanity, he still takes a positive attitude towards people."

Tutu has waltzed into modern life, teaching us to sing joyously in the face of ugly situations, for it is in the singing, in the continual gladness of being God's people, that we effectively change seemingly immovable objects into relics of the past, so that a new spirit rises. Tutu believes not only in the resurrection of Christ, but the resurrection of the downtrodden, whose faith and joy are not dominated by outside forces, but encouraged. The Archbishop will never give up, and he will never stop teaching, for in every lesson he hears the gospel of love for all the world clearly announced.

Do You Hear What I Hear?

> **Hearing,** *n. The process, function, or power of perceiving sound; the special sense by which noises, tones and utterances are received as stimuli through a characteristic organ, the ear; the auditory sense.*

> *For it is not the hearers of the law who are righteous before God, but the doers of the law who will be justified.* — *Romans 2:13*

> *. . . He who looks into the perfect law, the law of liberty, and perseveres, being no hearer that forgets but a doer that acts, he shall be blessed in his doing.* — *James 1:25*

Is it Erma Bombeck who coined the phrase, "A house divided against itself cannot stand one another?" Beyond the roar of the trunk-sized ghetto blaster shouldered by the high schooler sauntering down Main Street and the neighbor's college-age daughter's stereo broadcasting to six square blocks of the neighborhood, there is an island of quiet in which 22 little six-year-olds truly love each other, an undivided house in which the small fry can truly stand one another just fine.

They say "please" and "thank you," "you're welcome," and "excuse me" without reminders and greet adults with sincere words of welcome. If you believe such a classroom is an impossibility, it's not. They're youngsters who were taught how to listen. "Listen for what you want to hear," said the teacher. But it was not listening to others, twisting their terms and reshaping their vocabularies, that she was after. They were to listen to themselves make the necessary corrections. Before long, they were not only hearing themselves accurately, but others also.

James advised his readers, "Let every man be quick to hear, slow to speak, slow to anger, for the anger of man does not work the righteousness of God (1:19-20)."

Jesus was one who was quick to hear. When Jesus heard that John the Baptist had been arrested by Herod, he himself filled the leadership void and echoed John's call to repent (Matthew 4:12ff). When he heard John had been maliciously decapitated, his heart sought a lonely place to meditate as he grieved (Matthew 14:13). When at Capernaum Jesus heard the Roman centurion's explanation of the role of authority, he marveled at the man's insight, saying, "I tell you, not even in Israel have I found such faith (Luke 7:1ff)." He heard the whisperings of his detractors, and reminded them, "Those who are well have no need of a physician, but those who are sick. Go and learn what this means, 'I desire mercy, not sacrifice.' For I came not to call the righteous, but sinners (Matthew 9:10-13)." He listened carefully to the wealthy synagogue ruler who sought eternal life. "One thing you still lack," he said and then begged him to reconsider his priorities and follow him. But the man refused. Evidently he didn't hear Jesus clearly speak about the "treasure in heaven" that would be his (Luke 18:18ff).

Jesus heard. He listened well. He heard Bartimaeus, the blind man, sitting by Jericho's gate crying for help, when others rebuked him to keep silent. He gave him his sight (Mark 10:46ff). Another blind man whom he healed, this one in Jerusalem, was cast out of the synagogue because of it. Jesus, upon hearing that, searched for the healed man and revealed himself as the Messiah, rewarding him with what the whiners sought themselves (John 9:1ff). He evidently heard the inner longings of a hungry crowd when he preached three days on a mountain slope, and knew they were famished. Compassionately, he arranged for their miraculous lunch (Matthew 15:32ff). He heard his mother when she referred Cana's wine problem to him. He must have heard the widow of Nain's inner prayers about her dead son (Luke 7:11ff). And Mary and Martha about Lazarus (John 11:1ff). Jesus possessed perceptive hearing, keen hearing, compassionate hearing.

He heard everything. He heard the hosannas of the throngs lining the route from Bethany over the Mount of Olives to Jerusalem. He heard the screeching squawks of the murderous rejecters: "Crucify him! Crucify him!"

But most of all, he heard the cry of the sinful from Eden to Calvary, from creation to crucifixion, and he hears us yet. He heard what he needed to hear, our deepest longing. And we have heard from his deeper love.

That's the message the Christian school puts across best. It's not having the world's greatest library that does it, or possessing innumerable electronic teaching aids. What does it is when the teachers and staff speak love so loudly in their silent serving that no one fails to hear its implications for themselves.

Do you hear what I hear? We are to be doers, not just hearers; lovers not just livers.

It's Jesus speaking through you that enables others to hear his gospel.

Paul

Late-blooming Teacher

So Barnabas went to Tarsus to look for Saul; and when he had found him, he brought him to Antioch. For a whole year they met with the church, and taught a large company of people; and in Antioch the disciples were for the first time called Christians.　　　*Acts 11:25-26*

Now in the church at Antioch there were prophets and teachers, Barnabas, Symeon who was called Niger, Lucius of Cyrene, Manaen a member of the court of Herod the tetrach, and Saul. While they were worshiping the Lord and fasting, the Holy Spirit said, "Set apart for me Barnabas and Saul for the work to which I have called them." Then after fasting and praying they laid their hands on them and sent them off.　　　*— Acts 13:1-3*

While the words of Luke surge like the surf, quickly peaking, rapidly washing ashore, and then disappearing into the mind's sand, while the foam and fuss of another wave tumble quickly behind it, there are, actually, often long gaps between the waves he describes. The story of Paul is one of those with gigantic dips between the swells. Following his conversion enroute to Damascus, the learned rabbi spent some three years being tutored by the Lord in the desert of Arabia (Galatians 1:17-18; 1 Corinthians 15:3). Then he went to Jerusalem to meet with the disciples, but "they were all afraid of him, for they did not believe that he was a disciple (Acts 9:26). Repudiated by the leadership, rejected by the faithful, Saul went home to Tarsus disillusioned, we can imagine, which is evidenced by the fact nothing happened in the next seven years of any great importance. He had been discarded, abandoned, ignored like so much kelp piled upon the beach of time. Barnabas, who attempted to weave him into the warp and woof of the apostles, had no success. He, too, forgot about the man of Tarsus.

Until . . . until he couldn't carry on by himself any longer. Barnabas needed help, trained help, strong help, a partner of deep faith, one who had experienced the gospel in all its intellectual importance as well as its pragmatic spiritual assurances. He reached out for Saul, traveling the distance from Antioch of Syria to Tarsus on foot, over 100 miles away. To some, it may have seemed a wasted decade until then, but what followed was so much more powerful because the arrogant Saul was able to endure the humiliation without losing faith. Instead, he grew. The rough edges were smoothed; his feisty spirit tempered a bit. We know of nothing that happened during those ten years in "retirement," as James Kallas terms the era between conversion and consecration, except that Saul was marinating in the juices of his own experiences of Christ.

Paul was a late-bloomer, but what a bouquet he produced. It was because one man did not forget him. Peter and John did not offer encouragement, nor Thomas, nor James (with whom he visited in Jerusalem) nor the rest. But Barnabas did. He was like Mendelssohn when the world forgot Bach; he brought him out of mothballs with such an unforgettable rendition that Mendelssohn was surpassed. So it was for Barnabas. It did not take Saul long to come to full flower. Before the end of the first missionary journey, not only did his name change to Paul, but the leadership role was gladly given over to the man of Tarsus by his brother missionary (Acts 13:9, 13). Barnabas knew he had been God's ally in the enlistment of Paul for exceptional service.

There are all too many shelf Christians lying fallow like an unused Saul who require a Barnabas to restore them to their rightful leadership roles.

Which parents of past students are stored in a Tarsus cupboard? What students, no longer enrolled, could be Sauls waiting to become Pauls? What members of the congregation are deposited in some apostolic warehouse, neglected and forgotten, but still ready reserves to augment the work of teaching Christ? What aging recipient of some other Damascus Road enlightenment is exiled from the mainstream of ministry, rejected (not dejected), who could be drawn into missionizing your class, evangelizing your neighborhood for new students, or building up the Body of Christ in some other way?

A confirmand's sermonette was put aside for more than a decade. When she was married, however, her unchurched husband resisted her efforts to become involved in her faith. That little witness of the past, however, had not lost its power. It was prepared in a time of great spiritual growth. She took it out of the family archives and let it witness once more in its original fervor. He acquiesced, saying, "If this Christ means this much to you, I want to serve him, too."

Late-bloomers can still be dazzlers. Like Saul or Bach or a witness now put aside.

Will you be the Barnabas, the Mendelssohn, the young bride, to call these closeted Christians back to your Antioch?

Holding Back A River

River, *n. A natural stream of water larger than a brook or a creek.*

And while all Israel were passing over on dry ground, the priests who bore the ark of the covenant of the Lord stood on dry ground in the midst of the Jordan, until all the nation finished passing over the Jordan.
— *Joshua 3:17*

An elementary school teacher from Olivette, Missouri, was attending a convention. Standing near the book display, she talked with two others. "If I were to write a book," she said, her eyes emphasizing her eagerness, "I would title it *Five Minutes after Recess* or *It's Not My Fault*." It sounded to me like someone trying to hold back a river with wisdom ensconced in humor. Whether it was the water dividing Egypt from Sinai at the time of the Exodus, or that river separating the wilderness wanderings from the Promised Land as Joshua led them home, God was the one who stopped the flow and let his people stream across. And so it is that God can still hold back a river.

Dr. Oscar Feucht, a leader in Christian family education wrote in *Helping Families through the Church* nearly 35 years ago, "Families are in distress in every part of the world." He echoed a list by Louise Bracher of threats to the family then, which seem little different today.

His echoes include such items as economic, religious, legal props, divorce, sexual associations, society's stress on success, unrealistic romance and happiness goals, changing standards of sexual behavior, separating members of the family in our society, population mobility, inadequate housing, and the moving of religious training outside the home.

Other areas of concern include lessening parental controls, competition from television, radio, and schools that interferes with the raising of children, and change that brings emotional strains and tensions on all families.

How can we hold back such a flood?

We can't, not by ourselves. But just as we must deal pragmatically with the first five minutes after recess, so we must not feel guilty because all of these forces seem to interplay in our classrooms simultaneously. Instead, we do well to follow the Israelite marchers as they pass by the ark of the covenant in midstream. God held back the flood then, and we can seek him to continue to do so now, or ask him to teach us how to handle the overflowing banks of difficulty.

In her book *Don't Shoot the Dog! The New Art of Teaching and Training,* Karen Pryor emphasizes the need for positive reinforcement, which she describes as "anything which, occurring in conjunction with an act, tends to increase the probability that the act will occur again." It's a theory she applies to animal training, human beings, and problem management of all sorts.

In short, holding back rivers today, whether social mores or spiritual Jordans, requires us to cultivate the same quality of relationship with God that enabled Israel to march across the waters on dry land. That's a very positive reinforcement, faith! And it is much easier now than then, because we know Jesus. Instead of eying merely the problem, look to the promise. "I am the way, the truth, and the life," said our Lord. "No one comes to the Father, but by me (John 14:6)." This is more than positive thinking. It is faith that deals forcefully with possibilities in Christ.

If we can't face up to all of the threats Louise Bracher lists, we can deal with the first five minutes after recess. That accomplishment will help us collectively to reinforce positively other aspects of life that will hold back the river threatening us.

And we won't even have to write a book about it. It's been done.

Mother Teresa Of Calcutta

A Rich Compassion For The World's Poor

*". . . for I was hungry and you gave me food, I was
a stranger and you welcomed me, I was naked and you
clothed me, I was sick and you visited me, I was in prison
and you came to me . . ."*　　　— *Matthew 25:35-36*

He is a diminutive professor in size, but a giant in thought
and faith. Dr. B. Srinivasa Murthy, a graduate of the University of Mysore in India, and the University of Mainz in Germany, is a philosopher, a Christian, who teaches with depth
and conviction. It is no surprise to learn he had returned to
his native India to discover the immense courage of "the saint
of the gutters," Mother Teresa of Calcutta.

It was fascinating to hear his personal appraisal in private
conversation, then to hear him lecture about his experiences
in visiting this remarkable woman, and finally to read his careful analysis in his book, *Mother Teresa and India*. Here was
a teacher who wanted to learn, a teacher who wanted to pass
on the lessons gained. He says, "Meeting Mother Teresa has
been a very rewarding spiritual experience and, undoubtedly,
my faith has been strengthened. In fact, it has been an unforgettable highlight in my life."

Why is this Albanian-born Yugoslavian woman worldrenown? A nun who taught in a Roman Catholic high school
in Calcutta for 20 years, eventually becoming its principal, was
not content with teaching only the well-to do. She received "a
call within a call to help the poor, while living among them,"
she says. Here she would become the student, and the poorest
of the poor would teach her many lessons, which she, in turn,
would share with the world.

Like Japan's Toyohiko Kagawa, she would work in the
slums. He ministered in the tenements of Kobe called
Shinkawa, said to be the worst slums in the world, and there
made discoveries that led to social improvements for the

whole Japanese nation. If Mother Teresa's vast impact has not changed Calcutta's ghastly slums as completely as Kagawa did Japan, she has had an even greater influence on the world. When she received the Nobel Peace Prize in 1979, she did so "in the name of the hungry, of the naked, of the homeless, of the blind, of the lepers, of all those who feel unwanted, unloved, uncared for throughout society." Since that time, she has broadened her work far beyond Calcutta with projects in other nations. Among the poorest of the poor in the far-reaching ministry she and the Missionaries of Charity have developed are those suffering from AIDS.

And what does she teach us?

First, she gives up on no one. In the most debraggled beggar she finds the beckoning eyes of Christ, calling her to serve. There are so many children whose parents cannot or will not pay attention to them that teachers become surrogate parents, providing encouragement, giving assistance, elevating the poorest of the poorest students to a place of being wanted and cherished and motivated to be more than ignored and lonely children. When a reporter asked Mother Teresa if the sisters in her order ever suffered "burnout," she did not know what the word meant. When it was explained to her, she answered that the sisters never suffer burnout because the poor "give us so much more than we give them." Give up on no one and discover the rewards.

Second, she will not retire. Born in August, 1910, she has reached what some call "the golden years," but to her they are filled with the golden glow of opportunity. Age has not changed her keen dedication to her mission. Illness has forced her into hospitalization a time or two, but it has always resulted in her returning to her duties to the world's neglected souls. Never abandon your mission, the singular call God has given. There are more opportunities ahead.

Third, poverty is no obstacle to success. She has committed herself to poverty, to dwelling with the poor in the tenements of Calcutta, but she has also, despite her own financial poverty, built a home for the dying (Nirmal Kriday), a children's home (Shishu Bhavan) for infants left on the streets to die, and a leper colony (Shanti Nagar, which means "City of Peace"). More than 100 centers are operated by the Missionaries of Charity in India, and the poor in at least 52 other countries now being served in 213 houses. Leadership in stewardship is the gift Mother Teresa brings to the world, and the world is responding. She says, "You have to do it as if everything depends on you — but leave the rest to God." All things are possible to the believer, taught Jesus (Mark 9:23).

Fourth, once God has called you, never doubt your mission is his mission. "I have never had a doubt," she says. "But I am convinced that it is he and not I. That it is his work, and not my work. I am only at his disposal. Without him I can do nothing. But even God could do nothing for someone already full. You have to be completely empty to let him in to do what he will. That's the most beautiful part of God, eh? Being almighty, and yet not forcing himself on anyone." Refreshment in God's Word, time for reflection, spiritual growth, prayer and contemplation, and sacraments empower this tiny woman for a giant ministry. She has said, "If all of us spent a little more time on our knees in prayer to God, we would then begin to love. If you love, you cannot hurt anyone." "The fruit of faith is always love," she reminds us. "The fruit of love is action. We put our love for Jesus in a living action."

Last, keep the door open to a nurtured faith. When Dr. Murthy asks Mother Teresa "How is it possible to have unshakable faith in God all the time and serve him singlemindedly?" she responded, "Just as we need food to nourish our body, we need holy communion to strengthen the spirit. The more regularly we receive it, the more strength we get." She emphasizes, "My life is interwoven with the eucharist. We do not do just social work — we are contemplative sisters working among the poorest of the poor."

Despite the immensity of the problem, the sheer numbers of starving, lonely, ailing people in the world, Mother Teresa of India is undaunted. She is a teacher who has learned well from Christ. Dr. Murthy and other professors like him who have gone to the sources for insight have also found nourishment. The condition of some of the sick was so repugnant to him, he could barely stay where they were, marveling, however, at the loving care of the sisters, who were not revolted by the decaying flesh of those they served, or the nauseating sores they tended. They provided the poorest of the poor with the wealth of the wealthiest of all, with the love of God.

Verbalizing Virtue

Voice, *n. Sound uttered by living beings, esp. by human beings in speech or song, crying, shouting, etc. Faculty or power of utterance; speech.*

. . . Speaking the truth in love, we are to grow up in every way into him who is the head, into Christ, from whom the whole body, joined and knit together by every joint with which it is supplied, when each part is working properly, makes bodily growth and upbuilds itself in love. — *Ephesians 4:15-16*

There are times when I'm certain that I have been caught up into the third heaven. It happens Wednesdays, when we have our school chapel service and the children sing. It happens Thursdays, when Sharron Bonea directs the older classes' music period with Barbara Torgerson accompanying. My office is 40 feet away, but I can hear the celebrative singing. Outside my window, the children play. There are shouting and screaming, cheers and encouragements, at recess and lunchtime. The day care program takes place in Selbo Hall outside my office door, so I hear the sounds of voices from seven in the morning until school time and afterward until six. All of its bubbling, giddy sounds lift my soul heavenward.

Somehow in that babble I hear the whole school speaking the truth in a jubilant love that does not become stagnant, though it is repeated daily. There are rare occasions when the noise level in Selbo Hall exceeds that of a rock concert, but that happens usually when inclement weather makes playing outside impossible. I know how much I enjoy the youthful voices when summer vacation comes and the children disappear from the premises. I miss the exultant sound of their giggles and gushings, the gay greetings they give to each other, and the animated conversations of girls playing with dolls and boys buzzing around on turtle trikes.

But a voice must be more focused than merely to gush.

Surely reading isn't learned by permitting garbled sounds, whether that's the voice of the reader or the teacher. Nor is math taught simply by jamming a workbook in the student's hand. The art of speaking makes the instrument of the voice a tool for understanding, for learning and teaching others. No wonder Paul underscores our need to speak the truth in love. Without love, it becomes a distortion.

While it's a sitcom, the reason *The Golden Girls* get along so well is that love binds the foursome together, despite their consistent putdowns. It's a secular show, but the characters portray love. They can verbalize virtue, as well as vanities, venom and verities. They can vindicate and are seldom vindictive. Sophia and Rose are opposite poles, while Dorothy represents logic and Blanche romance, if somewhat bawdy. They communicate their respect and voice their views.

"I thought you weren't speaking," said a parent to an eight-year-old, when she found her playing with a friend with whom she had a flap.

"Oh, that was when we didn't have anything to say to eacher other, but now she's been to the beach, and I saw *Batman*."

How much greater is the communication between those who can verbalize virtue, who can speak of life without the vulgarities of the movies and the foul speech of the marketplace. It isn't that they must quote Scripture, or piously invoke God's name repeatedly, but they recognize that they speak the same language, a language, like the children's songs, that comes closer to heaven than hell.

We have something important to discuss. It may seem less urgent than reducing the nuclear arsenal or achieving *glasnost* and *perestroika,* simply because it's not on the nightly news, but what will fuel these important steps to beneficial fruition is a world that speaks the truth in love, that grows up into Christ, and celebrates the unity he provides by hymning him in praises sung aloud, as well as prayers for one another, quietly uttered.

Let your voice declare God's grace as you go over nature's geography, for it is this aspect of the geography of the teacher, the voice, that will enable a child to find his or her way through today's jungle. Speak a word of hope.

Thomas

Scuttling Titles

Thomas, called the Twin, said to his fellow disciples,
"Let us also go, that we may die with him."
— *John 11:16*

They tagged him "the Doubter," and he was, but that was only an incident, a momentary frailty in a lifetime of service. He was also faithful. They hung a title on him and it endured. They carefully boxed him into a neat little package of disbelief, when that was not it at all. How quickly we peg people with nicknames that are undeserved.

A husky kid of my youth was called "Cow," and it stuck. Another student they named "Squirrel," for his glasses and large eyes, and it never changed. A young lady with a weight problem was designated "Heavy Evvie." Such names may identify a person for a time, but is it fair? Thomas was a doubter once, but both before and after that event Thomas was a believer.

Abraham was known as the "friend of God," says James (3:23). Jesus himself said to his disciples, "No longer do I call you servants . . . but I have called you friends (John 15:15)." Here is the term the teacher needs, as well as the student, the title that enriches rather than enrages, the claim of being God's friend in Christ, and their friend, too.

It was Thomas, when Jesus was about ready to make his final visit to Jerusalem, to the thick of the cauldron of Pharisaic hatred and plotting by high priests and the sanhedrin, who proved to be Jesus' closest friend. It was not Peter nor John, but Thomas. "Let us also go, that we may die with him," he said.

It's easy to pigeon-hole doubters and negativists, Republicans and Democrats, penny-pinchers and extravagant spenders, but these views may be only part of the picture, inaccurate and mistaken.

77

A child, unnerved by an IQ test, flopped. He was called dumb, but the teacher took time to get acquainted and discovered him to be bright. A sixth-grade girl proved herself insensitive and brutal, but when this layer was peeled back, they found a volatile force that could be channeled into positive, loving action. A teacher was said to be totalitarian in the classroom until he was allowed to become a friend by a youngster who saw beyond the bluster. There is always another side to a derogatory name.

Thomas, tradition tells us, went on to India proclaiming the gospel. Surely, to call him "the Doubter" any longer is to misjudge an apostle with enormous faith.

One teacher makes the habit of trying to see the other side every time she characterizes a student, a neighbor, a colleague with a negative name. She purposely looks for more positive qualities. Invariably, she finds them. "I have decided for every dirty name a person received, there is an opposite, more beautiful one to be mined." She searches for the motherlodes and finds innumerable nuggets of glistening gold.

If we're willing to go with the one subject to name-calling, as Jesus was with Thomas, will we not discover a friend? What will die is the undeserved designation. What will live is Christ in the midst of us, sharing his love, so that we can love even the unlovely fully.

Greening Valleys

Valley, *n. An elongated depression, usually with an outlet, between bluffs, or between ranges of hills or mountains.*

Thou makest springs gush forth in the valleys; they flow between the hills, they give drink to every beast of the field; the wild asses quench their thirst. By them the birds of the air have their habitation; they sing among the branches. From thy lofty abode thou waterest the mountains; the earth is satisfied with the fruit of thy work. Thou dost cause the grass to grow for the cattle, and plants for man to cultivate, that he may bring forth food from the earth, and wine to gladden the heart of man, oil to make his face shine, and bread to strengthen man's heart. — Psalm 104:10-15

I live and serve in two splendid valleys. The one is called Blossom Valley, because at one time it was filled with orchards of plum trees, cherries, and other fruit trees and provided a springtime vista. The other one is called Almaden Valley. It was rich with vineyards, zinfandel, chenin blanc, chardonay, and the like, while today it is planted with handsome homes, schools, and churches. These valleys are divided by a small ridge of mountains, yet all around us are other mountains, which provide for one large valley subdivided into lesser ones by hills.

While we never have snow on the valley floor that lasts more than a few minutes, several times a year the mountains will be dusted, sometimes quiet heavily, and the panorama is exceptionally exhilarating, and can last for several days. But it is as the wintry rains are at their peak that the valleys begin to erupt from their dismal seasonal darkness into shimmering places of rapturous beauty. Streets are lined with flowering trees, and yards burst into such an array of color that one thinks it's a movie set. The brown and gold hills turn kelly green and shades of Chinese jade, yellow-green at first and then maturing into hues of blue-green and emerald as the season progresses, and we dwell in a wonderland that only God could make. Sometimes the blue lupin or California poppies' vivid safron yellow punctuates the greening process with their effulgent hues.

Isn't every child a greening valley, small like a hidden vale, yet surrounded by defensive hills, requiring an explorer to probe for a pass that will allow the teacher to send in loads of seed for planting? Shouldn't every student be seen as a greening place, where God can sow his wonder and harvest many a future crop? Shouldn't the Christian school be the place for planting and reaping, for cultivating and nurturing? That means every teacher needs to keep the green thumb green.

Garfield, Jim Davis' comic cat, discovers the beauties of spring as he was attempting to kick his "industrial-strength depression." Not content with a Maalox moment, he went leaping through the wildflowers and dashing through the tulips and daffodils. Garfield was suddenly seized by gratitude. "Mother Nature," he purrs, "If you had a body and a face, I'd give you a hug and a kiss."

The psalmist expressed his joy in the fruitful capacity of the valley in a way that teachers can share. He sees not only what they are, but what they can provide.

That means the green thumb needs to stay green.

Lorena Pepper Edlen tells the story of driving alongside the Franklin Mountains in New Mexico one spring day that changed her life from despair to a crescendo of joy. Her son had just been divorced and her daughter-in-law prohibited his family from seeing their two grandsons. Lorena was deeply depressed. They had prayed long, and others also, that this barrier would be lifted, but it wasn't budging. As she drove the highway, she suddenly went over the brow of a hill and saw an exhilarating sight in the valley just ahead. There before her were acres upon acres of luxuriant California poppies gilding the valley and the mountain slopes. She had never viewed such a glorious panorama before. Suddenly she remembered that 40 years earlier a local newspaper had sponsored a fund drive to buy poppy seeds to scatter throughout the area. An airplane had been used and pounds of seeds sown, but neither that spring nor any of the springs for 40 years had brought that grand crop of poppies to bloom. That winter, 40 years afterward, it had rained so thoroughly that not one of those latent poppy seeds could slumber any longer. It was a reminder that prayer can take time to be answered.

Keeping the green thumb means, keep on praying. Silent, brief prayers; oral, longer ones; those with perfect wording or those that tumble out in groans and grunts, all are prayers that God hears in the name of Christ. Not all prayers take 40 years to be answered. For the Christian teacher, many a prayer is answered in her children before the words are uttered. The valleys, the pupils, begin their greening often with a burst of chromatic swirls like poppies in full bloom, and one is made aware not only what valleys are for, but students as well. They're greening places meant to bear fruit.

Hidden among the rugged red hills of Edom's desert south of the Dead Sea is a valley lost for a thousand years. One enters it through the Siq, a narrow canyon several miles long, and stumbles upon a vast city that was the Nabataean capital. It's known as the red-rose city because of the color of the rock, but following the winter rains, that desert valley floor greens up with a lavish lushness that made it a major city in Old Testament times (known as *Sela*). This may have been the "Arabia" where Paul trained for three years following his conversion. At any rate, it vividly depicts for us how desolate valleys can become living places. Look for those potential greening places among students who need the benefits of a Christian school and enlist them as future Blossom Valleys.

Jean Calvin

The Call For A New Face

> *Stand therefore, having girded your loins with truth,*
> *and having put on the breastplate of righteousness, and*
> *having shod your feet with the equipment of the gospel*
> *of peace; above all taking the shield of faith, with which*
> *you can quench all the flaming darts of the evil one.*
> — *Ephesians 6:14-16*

From a distance, the Cathedral of St. Pierre in Geneva is plainly visible. As I ambled through the narrow lanes of the old city leading to this stately Gothic church in the chill of a stark January day, I kept looking for the indications I was nearing the distinguished structure where Jean Calvin preached with such zest. I came upon it from the south side and followed around the apse to the north transept, looking for an entrance, which was in the west end, I supposed. Then, because a cluster of houses and shops around the prominent landmark near its narthex blocked access, I had to find another way to the front of the church. When I got to a small square on the other side of that cluster, after finally finding a small street that entered it, I was certain the Gothic Church of St. Pierre should be there. What I found was not Gothic at all, but a Classical Revival facade. Greek columns with a pediment adorned the front of the structure. But surely, I thought, this must be St. Pierre. What else could it be? Daring to enter, I discovered that what seemed so strangely different from the front view was exactly the place I wanted to be.

Perhaps, in a way, that is what Calvin did for Christianity. While he seemingly put a different face on it, it was the same church as before the Reformation, but simplified of its elaborate trappings, its teachings better organized, its mission made more plain, its discipline emboldened.

Born July 10, 1509, the son of the secretary to the Bishop of Noyon, who was also the attorney for the cathedral chapter,

Calvin received his education in the same university as Erasmus, Rabelais, and Ignatius Loyola. In obedience to his father, and just the opposite of Luther, Calvin abandoned the study of theology to enter law. The application of his legal proclivities is readily evident in his writings and actions. The Reformation was sweeping Europe. France was not immune, and in the process young Calvin was captivated by its new facade, its open door to a Christianity bereft of its accumulated oddities. He saw the pristine faith of the apostles, and dreamed of a world in which the gospel was vigorously lived, where righteousness was evident in disciplined lives. His "sudden conversion," his scholarly and theological treatises that had bored some, excited others, and his move to Geneva by a circuitous route, much like my search for the door to St. Pierre, occupied several years. By 1536 Geneva declared itself in the camp of the Reformation. One writer has summarized that Calvin "shaped the ecclesiastical and civil affairs of Geneva during his lifetime and left his lasting imprint on its theology and ecclesiastical polity." He remained a popular figure in the city, except for the years between 1538 and 1541, when he was in exile in Strasbourg. Not everyone appreciated the clear new face Calvin was putting on the church and community life. The ideal of theocratic rule . . . God in charge of the city's morals . . . was intended to make Geneva a bit of heaven on erath, but instead it made it a locale of strictness and legalism. Such extreme severity was seen in the burning at the stake of an alleged heretic, Servetus, in 1553. Yet Calvin could counsel, "We have never been forbidden to laugh, or to be filled, or to join new possessions to old or ancestral ones, or to delight in musical harmony, or to drink wine."

But by and large, the scholarly Calvin left the world something more than an over-zealous eagerness for Christian morality and its discipline. He wrote, "Faith consists, not in ignorance, but in knowledge; and that, not only of God, but also of the divine will."

He was the consummate teacher. With all his other parish activities, Calvin remained a teacher, establishing an academy in 1559, where he taught theology. He insisted on putting a new face on the church by peeling back superstition and ignorance. "We should accustom ourselves to think of our position and work as sacred and well-pleasing to God, not on account of the position and work, but on account of the word and faith from which the obedience and work flow," wrote the reformer. The gospel had a lot to teach, thus he kept at it until death claimed him in 1564.

As I entered St. Pierre that chilly January Sunday, the congregation was singing a hymn. The preacher mounted the high pulpit afterward, and within minutes this French-speaking pastor was challenged by the voluminous howls of an infant so loud that the vast interior of that soaring nave seemed to rattle. Calmly he addressed the child, to the chuckles of the assembled congregation, and before long the serenity sought was happily gained, and the clergyman went on with his sermon. He, too, knew how to put a happy face on those crying out for needed changes. While Calvin certainly went about it differently, the original intention was the same, to please God and serve him well.

On Calvin's coat-of-arms is inscribed this motto, "My heart I give thee, Lord, eagerly and earnestly." That's the new face we need to put on every day, as well as one the church needs to wear, as well as those who teach in it.

Lin Yutang

Those Prodigals!

*We desire each one of you to show the same earnest-
ness in realizing the full assurance of hope until the end,
so that you may not be sluggish, but imitators of those
who through faith and patience inherit the promises.*
— *Hebrews 6:11-12*

The teacher is sometimes aware of the perceptive student who, later in life, repudiates the faith once eagerly upheld in youth. The proverb "Train up a child in the way he should go, and when he is old he will not depart from it (Proverbs 22:6)," is not fanciful nonsense, but an apt observation. Like the prodigal son, the wayward will often rebel for a time, but something, perhaps it is the forgiving father, or the remembrance of a home furnished with love, or their emptiness without a family's presence, draws them back.

Lin Yutang came home. He had wandered off to a foreign land, albeit it was his native land.

Born in 1895 in Fulkien Province in China to a Chinese Presbyterian pastor, Lin Yutang knew the marvels of a Christ-adoring home. He was a third generation Chinese Christian whose father dreamed of sending his bright son off to the leading universities to study. Perhaps it would be Berlin. Maybe Oxford. It was half a joke, half a serious hope. He studied in Shanghai first, and for the Christian ministry, hoping to follow in his father's footsteps.

"But other forces were at work to turn me toward paganism," he wrote later. In Peking, he discovered he was backward in Chinese folklore and thought. He plunged into the study of Chinese literature and philosophy, becoming a prodigal son in his own country. He put aside Christianity for Confucian ideals. He extolled humanism, "the belief in human reason and in man's power, lifting himself by his own bootstraps, to better himself and make a better world," as being the ideal. He was awash in its flood, until many years later he no longer saw humanism as enlightenment, for it leads directly to materialism. "Man's increasing belief in himself as God did not seem to be making him more godlike," reflecting the maturing philosopher.

Lin Yutang garnered degrees from Harvard, Jena, and Leipzig Universities and became a prominent essayist, often commenting on his new-found paganism. He lectured for a while at Peking, participated briefly in the Chinese revolutionary government, and took up residence in the United States, where he wrote voluminously and successfully on popular philosophy.

His wife, wherever they lived and whenever they traveled, went to church. "Sometimes I accompanied her," he writes. "More often than not I came away discouraged rather than inspired. I could not stand a second-rate sermon. I squirmed in my seat at the rantings I heard about sin, hellfire, and brimstone. I would resolve not to go again."

His wife did not take his resolution seriously. One Sunday in New York, she invited him to accompany her to Madison Avenue Presbyterian Church. She had prepared him by warning that he might not agree with the content of the sermon, but he could not help but be impressed by the literary quality and eloquence of the preacher. It was Dr. David Read who preached, but the message was straight from God. He returned to the awe-inspiring simplicity and beauty of the teachings of Jesus. Like Paul, he felt the "scales fall from my eyes."

"I found — as though I had never read of him before — that no one ever spoke like Jesus. He spoke of God the Father as one who knew him and was identified with him in the fullness of knowledge and love. No other teacher of men revealed such personal knowledge or such a sense of personal identity with God. The result was his astounding claim: 'He that has seen me has seen the father.' "

Lin Yutang found his way home. "Jesus speaks as the teacher who is master over both life and death. In him, this message of love and gentleness and compassion becomes incarnate. That, I saw, is why men have turned to him, not merely in respect but in adoration. That is why the light which blinded Paul on the road to Damascus with such sudden impact continues to shine unobscured and unobscurably through the centuries," wrote Lin Yutang in a 1959 magazine article titled, "Why I came Back to Christianity."

Lin Yutang is one of a host of Christians who forsook their Lord, wandering off to the far countries of philosophical adventurism, only to return eagerly and more emphatically to Christ. Malcolm Muggeridge is notable among them, as are C.S. Lewis and Evelyn Waugh and Alexander Solzhenitsyn and Martin Sheen.

Thus the teacher is challenged to keep more than the immediate future in view, the long haul, the pull up the hills of age and maturity. Will the faith fostered today enable a former student to "keep the faith" or return to it? Sow seeds carefully, because it may take decades for them to germinate. Prodigals are seeds that will inevitably come home when the winds of hope blow them back from that country afar off.

Jesus

The Incomparable Teacher

*A disciple is not above his teacher but everyone, when
he is fully taught, will be like his teacher.*

Luke 6:40

Jesus learned to teach at the feet of his earthly father, as
well as his heavenly one.

Was not Joseph, the Nazarene carpenter, attentive to God's
voice in his dreams? He was assured taking Mary as his wife
was right by an angel in a dream. He was told he could rescue
his family by fleeing to Egypt the night Herod's soldiers
pounced on the innocents in Bethlehem. Jesus could not help
but hear these stories of his birth, learning the importance of
every lesson. Had not the gifts of the magi provided the assets needed for that sojourn in a foreign land? Were not the
words of Simeon and Anna assurances of his role for the future? Joseph undoubtedly repeated these events over and over
again, teaching the youthful Jesus that his role would be to
teach and be salvation.

And the heavenly Father was in the midst of this earthly
teaching Joseph did, as well as in the synagogue, where God's
Word was shared, and in the wilderness, when God's enemy
sought to distract the son. Jesus was wonderfully taught so
that he could teach. And teach he did.

We can learn from him:

Prayer began and ended his day. Jesus was a superlative
teacher because he fortified himself in communion with his
father. It was not flippant praying or hasty words said quickly
driving the ancient freeways, but intensive prayers that listened
as well as spoke (cf Mark 1:35; Luke 3:21, 5:16, 6:12, 9:18,
28, 11:1).

Worship was part of his life. While daily devotions and
frequent preaching filled his week, Jesus was always at worship on the sabbath. Christian teachers who think their daily

91

experiences in Christian schools replace the necessities for regular Sunday worship have not learned that from Jesus (cf Luke 4:16, 6:1, Matthew 4:23, 12:9, Mark 6:2).

He dealt with people where they were. Erudition was simplified. He used pungent stories to illustrate profound truths. His parables were drawn from the resources his listeners knew well. They understood the implications readily. It was part of their culture. We still need to make deep thoughts understandable with current illustrations (cf his innumerable parables).

He did not ignore the hurting. He touched the blind, comforted the sorrowing, healed the sick and met their specialized needs. The hungry, he fed. The complaining, he confronted directly. If we cannot be Jesus, we can be like him, dealing directly with the troubled and the aching, the hateful and the hapless (cf Luke 6:17-19).

He taught individuals as well as vast crowds. His classroom was everywhere: along the roadside, in a field, on board a boat, on the mountainside, in a home, a synagogue, the temple, everywhere. While a well-equipped classroom is useful, a well-equipped teacher is far more important, for such a teacher never fails to instruct the student and/or the class immediately (cf Mark 10:1, Mark 6:44ff, 8:9ff, Luke 5:27ff, 6:1).

He prepared his students so well that the words could be recalled later and the lesson Jesus intended understood. That was true of both the crucifixion and the resurrection. Most of what we teach is being stored up like a recorded message to be played at a later time, when it is required (cf Matthew 26:75, Mark 14:72, Luke 22:61, 24:8, John 2:17, 22, 12:16).

Jesus utilized all of his emotions as means of teaching. One could hear his exuberance in his sermons and sense it in his conversations. His was not a monotone, flat, dull. He was not always mild-mannered, either. Remember the fury of his cleansing of the temple and the tears at Lazarus' graveside, the compassion when he saw the widowed mother at Nain and the hungering hordes on the mountainside? Remember also how he dealt with the Pharisees and the malcontents finding fault along the way. He could not turn the other cheek to a lie or distortion that would teach others the wrong lesson. Jesus was a vital person, animated, alive, a wise steward of all of his emotions. Teachers need to be in control of their emotions, but emotions need not be locked up inside.

Being frail imitations of Jesus is the best we can achieve, and yet is that not what he implies when he calls students to be like the teacher? Whatever teaching techniques gained in universities and colleges we employ, whatever contemporary tool from charts to computers we possess, emulating the greatest teacher of all is still the best way to instruct today's children.

For Jesus, it was not mechanical means, but enriching love. Is there a more effective way to clarify the important lessons of life?